School Is Closed

Written by Kathleen Fitzgibbon

Illustrated by Susan Banta

STECK-VAUGHN
COMPANY

A Division of Harcourt Brace & Company

Cleo and Leo Bear were twins. One cold
winter morning they opened their blinds.
Cleo blinked once. Leo blinked twice.

"Oh no!" they shouted. "It's snowing!"

"Look, school is closed again," said Cleo. Cleo and Leo looked at each other.

"What are we going to do all day?"

"I can't fly any planes today," said Dad.
"Why don't we go outside?"

"That is a good plan," said Mom. "Let's all
get set to go."

Cleo and Leo put on their fluffy coats and fluffy gloves. Cleo and Leo looked up at Dad.

"What are we going to do now?"

"Let's ride our sleds," said Dad.

"Cleo and Leo, flop down flat on your
sleds," said Dad. "Then slide down the slope.
Hold on, please!"

Cleo and Leo slid down the hill twice. Then they looked at Mom.

"What are we going to do now?"

"Let's build an igloo," said Mom. "There is plenty of snow."

"Look!" said Leo. "It's Twinky and Blinky and all our friends. They can help."

Everyone sliced blocks of snow and packed them into place. Cleo added a flag. Then she looked at Mom.

"What are we going to do now?"

"We will go ice skating," said Mom.

"The ice is slick," said Dad. "Be careful not to slip."

"It's so much fun to twirl and glide on the ice," said Leo. He looked at Cleo.

"What are we going to do now?"

"Let's make snow bears," said Cleo.

"We can use twigs for arms," said Leo.
"Then we can plop tall black hats on top."

"Our snow bears are twins, just like us," said Cleo. She looked at Leo.

"What are we going to do now?"

"We will build a fire in the fireplace," said Dad.

"Look at the fire blaze and the flames glow!" said Cleo.

The cold wind blew outside. "It was fun playing in the snow today," said Leo.

"What are we going to do now?"

"It's time to sleep," said Mom. "School will be closed again tomorrow." Cleo and Leo looked at each other.

"WHAT ARE WE GOING TO DO TOMORROW?"